Katharine Hepburn

A LIFE IN PICTURES

Katharine Hepburn

A LIFE IN PICTURES

by

DIANA KARANIKAS HARVEY & JACKSON HARVEY

MetroBooks

MetroBooks

An Imprint of Friedman/Fairfax Publishers

Library of Congress Cataloging-in-Publication Data

Harvey, Jackson.
    Katharine Hepburn / by Jackson Harvey and Diana
        Karanikas Harvey.
        p.   cm. — (A life in pictures)
    Filmography: p.
    Includes bibliographical references and index.
    ISBN 1-56799-566-7
    1. Hepburn, Katharine, 1909-   —Portraits. I. Harvey, Diana
        Karanikas.
II. Title. III. Series.
PN2287.H45H37 1998
791.43'028'092—dc21   97-34786

Editor: Francine Hornberger
Art Director: Jeff Batzli
Designers: Robert Brook Allen and Millie Sensat
Photography Editor: Amy Talluto
Production: Ingrid McNamara and Camille Lee

Color separations by Ocean Graphic International Company Ltd.
Printed in China by Leefung-Asco Printers Ltd.

1 3 5 7 9 10 8 6 4 2

For bulk purchases and special sales, please contact:
Friedman/Fairfax Publishers
Attention: Sales Department
15 West 26th Street
New York, NY 10010
212/685-6610   FAX 212/685-1307

Visit our Website:
http://www.metrobooks.com

To Marianthe and Cynthia Karanikas and Peter Harvey.

Acknowledgments

Special thanks to George Leis, Matt Leipzig, John and Sarah Harvey, Helen and Alexander Karanikas, Steve Slaybaugh, and Francine Hornberger.

CONTENTS

Introduction

A bove: "Well, I love you and you love me and that's that," were Kate's last words to the audience in her curtain speech for her last performance in *Coco*.

O pposite: Movie-star-to-be, Katherine Hepburn, as Tracy Lord, in a gown designed by Valentina for the 1939 Broadway production of *The Philadelphia Story*.

"After last night, there is a new star on the cinema horizon, and her name is Katharine Hepburn."

—The Hollywood Reporter *upon Hepburn's screen debut in* A Bill of Divorcement *(1932).*

Katharine Hepburn achieved a level of stardom that many actors strive for, but few attain. She appeared in more than forty motion pictures, six television movies, and some twenty-five stage productions. She brought to her roles a depth of character, an occasional eccentricity, and her distinctive New England Yankee accent, which set her apart from other leading ladies and established her as one of the most dynamic American actresses in motion picture history. Her work garnered her twelve Academy Award nominations for Best Actress, more than any other actress. She has won a record four Oscars—for *Morning Glory* (1933), *Guess Who's Coming to Dinner* (1967), *The Lion in Winter* (1968), and *On Golden Pond* (1981).

Her personal life, however, was fraught with turmoil and controversy. Born on May 12, 1907, Katharine Houghton Hepburn grew up in an idyllic setting, in Hartford, Connecticut, and at the Hepburn family's summer home at Fenwick on the Long Island Sound, a place she loved and would return to throughout her life. The daughter of a doctor and a suffragette, Kate had three brothers and two sisters. At the age of fourteen, her storybook childhood was forever altered when her sixteen-year-old brother Tom committed suicide by hanging himself. Kate discovered the body.

The tragedy did not destroy Kate. She grew up to be a strong person with an overwhelming life force. Katharine Hepburn was someone to be reckoned with. Her strong personality often led to conflicts and caused her to lose friends, while others, including directors George Cukor, John Huston, and George Stevens, remained her lifelong allies.

Hepburn began acting in amateur productions at age twelve and appeared in stage productions while in college at Bryn Mawr. She graduated in 1928 and set out to pursue acting in Baltimore with a letter of introduction to a local producer. That same year, she made her professional debut with a bit part in the play *The Czarina.* Before the year ended, she debuted on Broadway with a small part in *The Hostess.* For the next four years, she performed nearly nonstop in stage productions until her role in *The Warrior's Husband* in 1932 won her a motion picture contract with RKO Studios. In her first film,

A *Bill of Divorcement* (1932), she played opposite the legendary John Barrymore and instantly established herself as a leading lady. She won her first Academy Award for her role in *Morning Glory* (1933).

Despite her critical successes, many of Hepburn's films faltered at the box office. At one time, she was even labeled "box office poison" by the studios who refused to hire her. After being rejected for the role of Scarlett O'Hara in *Gone With the Wind*, Katharine packed her bags and moved back to Fenwick with hopes of returning to the stage. Her desires were not only met, but exceeded her expectations when her role as Tracy Lord in the Broadway production *The Philadelphia Story*, which opened in 1939, catapulted her straight back to Hollywood and to the pinnacle of stardom. She signed with MGM Studios for the film version of *The Philadelphia Story* (1940), which won the New York Film Critics' Award and garnered Hepburn an Academy Award nomination.

Hepburn's love life was tumultuous. She often chose troubled, enigmatic, intense men. She was married only once, to Ludlow Ogden Smith. They married in 1928 and divorced six years later. Her romantic liaisons included poet H. Phelps Putnam, wealthy entrepreneur Howard Hughes, and director John Ford, who at the time was married to another woman.

Her most notorious, and passionate love relationship was also with a married man, her longtime costar Spencer Tracy. Hepburn starred in *Woman of the Year* opposite Tracy. The chemistry between the two stars led to a string of films and some of Hepburn's most successful work. They performed in nine films together, including *Without Love* (1945), *State of the Union* (1948), *Adam's Rib* (1949), *Pat and Mike* (1952), and the last, made when Tracy was gravely ill, *Guess Who's Coming to Dinner* (1968).

Their affair began on the set of *Woman of the Year*, and continued for twenty-seven years. Tracy's mental state only intensified the turmoil of their relationship. He suffered from insomnia and had bouts of heavy drinking and amphetamine usage. Although Tracy never divorced his wife, Hepburn remained devoted to him until 1967, when he died from a heart attack at the age of sixty-seven. And it was Kate who found his body.

Katharine Hepburn was a private and elusive character, but her work speaks volumes. Many of her films, such as *The African Queen* (1951), *Suddenly, Last Summer* (1959), and *Long Day's Journey Into Night* (1962), are not just memorable, they are classics. Indeed, Hepburn herself is a classic: she is unique, she is timeless, she is movie magic.

Chapter One

Ingenue

Above: Katharine was born in Hartford, Connecticut, on May 12, 1907. The daughter of a successful surgeon, Dr. Thomas Norval Hepburn, and Katharine Houghton Hepburn, she was one of six siblings, pictured here in 1921 (from left to right): Kate, Marion (b. 1918), Bob (b. 1913), Katharine's mother with Peg (b. 1920), Tom (b. 1905), and Dick (b. 1911).

Opposite: In Katharine's senior year at Bryn Mawr College she was suspended for eight days for smoking in her room. She graduated in 1928 intent upon becoming an actress. Four days after receiving her diploma, she got her first role in the Baltimore production of *The Czarina*.

ight: Katharine has said of
her idyllic youth, "Mother
and Dad were perfect par-
ents. They brought us up with a
feeling of freedom. There were
no rules. There were simply
certain things which we did and
certain things which we didn't
do because they would hurt
others." Kate's mother with
children (clockwise) Kate, Bob,
Dick, and Tom.

Left: Kate (left) and her older brother Tom (right). Kate's idyllic childhood was shattered at fourteen when she discovered the body of her beloved brother Tom. He had hanged himself with bedsheets tied to the rafters. "People die—you cry—but inside I was frozen."

Below: Hepburn's family remained very close throughout the years. Here the other Hepburn women (left to right), Marion, mother Katharine, and Peg, attend the gala premier of *Alice Adams* in New York City, 1935.

Above: Katharine's mother was a leading suffragette and women's rights advocate. Seen here at a Philadelphia convention speaking on birth control, she often tackled controversial issues in a public forum.

Opposite: Kate performed in several Broadway productions until her huge success in *The Warrior's Husband* in 1932. Pictured here with Colin Keith-Johnstone, her role as Antiope caught the eye of a talent scout who worked for RKO, the Hollywood studio that would be the first to give her a movie contract.

Above: Katharine's acting endeavors began in earnest when she attended Bryn Mawr College. In the college production of *The Truth About Blayds*, Kate (second from right) played the male role of Oliver. Her first review in the *College News* called her "an engaging boy, roguish and merry." Her sister Marion (center) was also featured in the play.

Right: Hepburn's agent and on-and-off lover, Leland Hayward, was the scion of a socially prominent family of Philadelphia. He signed her following her work in the Broadway play *The Warrior's Husband*. While Katharine rejected his proposal of marriage, he remained her agent for many years.

Above: RKO Studios, Hollywood, California. Despite his personal dislike for Kate, legendary producer David O. Selznick, egged on by director George Cukor, gave Kate her first screen role in *A Bill of Divorcement* (1932). Afterward, he could not argue with the actress' successes and agreed to continue Hepburn's contract.

Opposite: Katharine starred opposite John Barrymore in her first film, *A Bill of Divorcement.*

Above: Kate in her second movie, *Christopher Strong* (1933), the story of a female aviator who falls in love with a married man, becomes pregnant by him, and commits suicide by pulling off her oxygen mask at 30,000 feet while going for the world altitude record.

"CHRISTOPHER STRONG"

with

KATHARINE HEPBURN

eft: *Christopher Strong's* director, Dorothy Arzner, did not like Hepburn and didn't want her to play the part of Lady Cynthia Darrington. She was forced to accept her only when her first choice, Ann Harding, became unavailable. Though the film was a box-office disappointment, the *Los Angeles Times* raved about Katharine, "Hepburn fascinates by her strange beauty and her inescapable magnetism."

ight: "You don't belong to any man now, you belong to Broadway!" was Adolph Menjou's famous line to Hepburn after her triumphant arrival at stardom for *Morning Glory*. Here Kate arrives for a private screening at Jesse Lasky's beach house in 1933 with Douglas Fairbanks, Jr.

Opposite: Two Hollywood legends: Douglas Fairbanks, Jr. and Katharine Hepburn embrace in *Morning Glory* (1933). Loosely based on the life of Tallulah Bankhead, the movie was a classic tale of a small-town girl who leaves home and returns a star. Only her third film, Hepburn won her first Academy Award for Best Actress.

Above: Hepburn and Fairbanks, Jr. in *Morning Glory* performing the balcony scene from *Romeo and Juliet.* According to Hepburn, Fairbanks, Sr. and Mary Pickford came to watch the filming when this scene was shot.

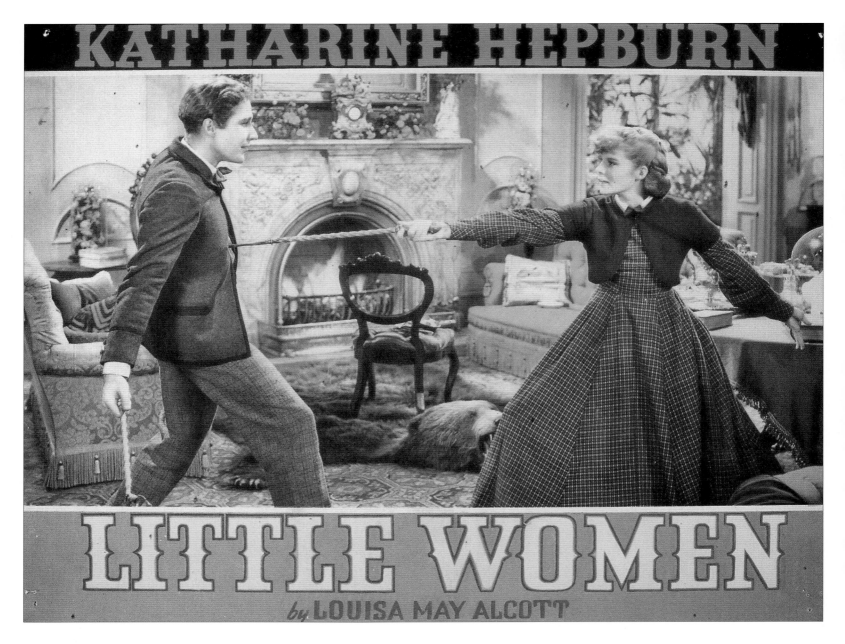

KATHARINE HEPBURN

LITTLE WOMEN
by LOUISA MAY ALCOTT

Above: Movie poster for the 1933 production of *Little Women*. This was the first time Hepburn attained solo star billing. She was also voted Best Actress at the 1934 Cannes Film Festival for her role as Jo. Sarah Y. Mason and Victor Herman won an Oscar for best screenplay and the picture received Academy Award nominations for Best Director and Best Picture.

Left: Hepburn (right) in a scene from *Little Women.* As her star rose in Hollywood, Kate highlighted her eccentricities. According to a gossip columnist, she allowed herself to be photographed without makeup, she dressed like a man, she distorted certain facts of her life in interviews, and she read her fan mail sitting on the curb outside the RKO lot. Still, critics and audiences raved about most of her performances.

Above: In 1933 Hepburn reunited with George Cukor (right) to play Jo in *Little Women.* Here Cukor directs Kate and Douglas Montgomery, who played Laurie. "Like Garbo and Camille, she was born to play Jo. She's tender and funny, fiercely loyal, and plays the fool when she feels like it. There's a purity about her. Kate and Jo are the same girl: you could go with whatever she did on the set…"

Above: *Spitfire* (1934) is the story of Trigger Hicks, a young tomboy and faith-healer who comes down from the Ozark Mountains to kidnap a neglected baby and falls in love with an engineer—an odd role, even by Hepburn standards. A taste of the unflattering reviews to come (which only strengthened her spirit), *The New York Post* said her southern accent "is pitched somewhere between Amos and Andy and is no more convincing than either."

Left: Despite her many successes in Hollywood, Hepburn was never really at home there. "Whenever possible I always went back East to my family, to the place where I'd lived when I was one, two, three, and so on. And I know that's where I began and where I'll be buried...."

Chapter Two

Leading Lady

Above: Kate poses for a publicity photo for *The Philadelphia Story* with (left to right) Cary Grant, Jimmy Stewart, and John Howard. Of her performance, *Life* magazine wrote: "...when Katharine Hepburn sets out to play Katharine Hepburn, she is a sight to behold. Nobody is then her equal."

Opposite: Cary Grant and Katharine Hepburn in *Holiday* (1938). Said Grant, "Working with Kate Hepburn was incredible." Said Hepburn of Grant, "He's a delicious personality who has learned to do certain things marvelously well."

R ight: The 1930s was a decade of growth and change for Hepburn. The diversity of her work and the chances she took were sometimes perplexing, often daring. She would not take the easy road to stardom.

B elow: In 1933, Kate returned to Broadway to appear in *The Lake*. Receiving mixed reviews from critics, her performance prompted the now-infamous quip from Dorothy Parker, "Miss Hepburn ran the gamut of emotions from A to B."

Above: Katharine Hepburn, movie star, poses for the paparazzi on the SS *Paris* on her trip back to New York after an extended vacation in Europe in 1934.

R ight: Kate, accompanied by her secretary, Laura Harding, walks by reporters flocking to photograph her upon her return from Mexico in 1934.

B elow: Hepburn returned to Hollywood in 1934 to film *The Little Minister*. Here, she films a scene with costar John Beal while director Richard Wallace (third from left) and crew look on.

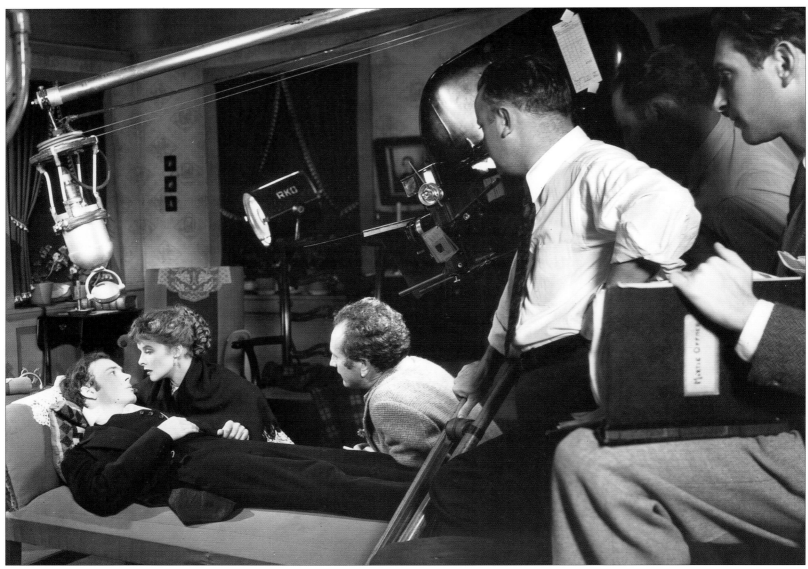

Above: Katharine's sixth film, *The Little Minister* (1934), was not a success. After two consecutive movie flops, Pandro S. Berman (then head of RKO production) said of Hepburn, "I realized that Kate wasn't a movie star. She wasn't going to become a star either...." Hepburn would eventually prove him wrong.

Opposite: Considered to be the low point of her RKO career, Hepburn starred with Charles Boyer in *Break of Hearts* (1935), a melodramatic love story with a very silly plot and nonsensical dialogue.

Above: Directed by George Cukor, *Sylvia Scarlett* (1935) marked the first of four films Hepburn would make with Cary Grant. In the film, Kate played a young girl posing as a boy in a gang of London thieves.

Opposite: Kate and Fred McMurray in *Alice Adams* (1935). After three successive flops, *Alice Adams* was an exhilarating success and one of the best of the films she made at RKO. Hepburn's portrayal of Alice also earned her a second Oscar nomination.

Above: Hepburn in her dressing room with Mortimer Offner, who cowrote (with Dorothy Yost) the screenplay for *Alice Adams*, based on Booth Tarkington's novel.

Right: Director George Cukor, who worked with Hepburn on many films, was one of her best friends and remained so throughout her career. She would often attend soirées at his house with other entertainment industry friends. From left, Andy Lawler, Hepburn, Roland Leigh, and William Haines enjoy each other's company around Cukor's pool.

Above: Katharine in the title role in *Mary of Scotland* (1936). Based on the play by Maxwell Anderson, the film received high critical acclaim. Hepburn had a brief but intense love affair with the director, the legendary John Ford.

elow: *Quality Street* (1937), directed by George Stevens and co-starring Franchot Tone, was a soap opera set during the Napoleonic wars. Even though she had risen to stardom at this point, Kate still had her share of bad reviews. *The New York Times* declared, "[Hepburn's] Phoebe Throssel needs a neurologist far more than a husband. Such flutterings and jitterings and twitchings, such hand-wringings and mouth quaverings, such runnings-about and eyebrow-raisings have not been seen on the screen in many a moon."

Above: In *A Woman Rebels* (1936), Hepburn played a feminist in Victorian England. From left, Herbert Marshall, Elizabeth Allan, Van Heflin, and Hepburn.

Left: Kate and director George Stevens in 1937. Stevens was unknown when he was hired to direct *Alice Adams*, but he would become one of the most successful motion picture directors of this era.

Opposite: Katharine Hepburn and Ginger Rogers in *Stage Door* (1937). It was in this film that Hepburn utters her famous quote, "The calla lilies are in bloom again. Such a strange flower, suitable to any occasion. I carried them on my wedding day, now I place them here in memory of something that has died."

Opposite: The golfing scene in *Bringing Up Baby* (1938) where socialite Susan Vance (Hepburn) first meets and falls in love with paleontologist David Huxley (Cary Grant). This was the pair's second film together. It was while golfing with Grant that Hepburn first met Howard Hughes. Hughes landed his plane on the fairway of the Riviera Country Club and joined them to play the back nine; it was the first date of Hughes' and Hepburn's legendary Hollywood love affair.

Above: *Bringing Up Baby* marked the end of Kate's career at RKO. Branded "box-office poison" by the Theater Owners of America (despite the fact that her performances and films were mostly well received), Hepburn bought out her contract. In this scene, David and Susan beg George the dog to show them where he's buried David's intercostal clavicle—a dinosaur bone.

Right: David and Susan trudge through a lake in a neverending search for Huxley's "rare and precious bone." Despite the film's charm, Hepburn's career was slowly sinking.

Right: Kate rehearses a scene from *The Philadelphia Story* with Jimmy Stewart and Ruth Hussey as director George Cukor looks on. Hepburn, Stewart, and Cukor were all nominated for Academy Awards.

Opposite (top): In 1938, at the age of 31, Hepburn returned to New York City, convinced her career was over. Soon after, playwright Philip Barry (Holiday) told Hepburn he'd written a role for her, Tracy Lord in the Broadway production of *The Philadelphia Story*. Shown here on stage with Joseph Cotton, Hepburn waived her salary, put up one-quarter of the production costs, and bought the film rights to the play. The gamble paid off; she made $500,000 from the stage production and relaunched her Hollywood career.

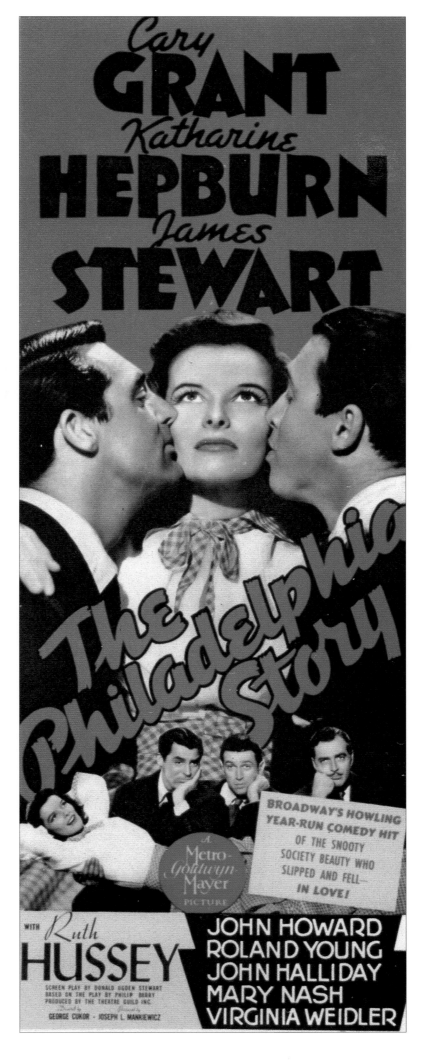

Left: The film version of *The Philadelphia Story* (1940) marked the beginning of Hepburn's MGM years. George Cukor was signed as director at Hepburn's request. Kate wanted Spencer Tracy and Clark Gable to play opposite her, but when they refused, she settled for James Stewart and Cary Grant.

Below: "There's a magnificence in you, Tracy!... You're the golden girl, full of life and warmth and delight!" exclaims reporter and love interest Mike Connor (James Stewart) in *The Philadelphia Story*. Stewart won an Academy Award for his performance.

Opposite: Cary Grant (as C.K. Dexter Haven) and Hepburn (as Tracy Lord) in *The Philadelphia Story*. By the end of the film, Tracy has decided to remarry her ex-husband, Dexter, instead of her fiance or her brief love interest, Mike Connor.

A bove: Kate with Virginia Weidler and Roland Young in *The Philadelphia Story.*

O pposite: Years later, *The Philadelphia Story* was still popular enough to warrant a radio presentation. Here, Hepburn, Grant, and Stewart clown around during a break in a 1947 broadcast.

In the span of seven years, Hepburn saw her career go in the tank (left) then skyrocket back to the pinnacle of stardom (below). She would stay at the top for the rest of her career.

Opposite: Kate at President Franklin D. Roosevelt's home in Hyde Park, New York, in 1940. The president's son, Elliott, serves chowder. Hepburn was one of many notables who gathered at Hyde Park to plan a radio show in support of FDR's policies.

Chapter Three

Star

Above: Hepburn in an MGM publicity shot from the 1940s.

Opposite: *Keeper of the Flame* (1942), directed by George Cukor, was a melodrama in which Hepburn starred as a widow who tries to prevent a journalist (Spencer Tracy) from discovering that her husband had been a Fascist.

Woman of the Year (1942) was the first of nine successful films that starred Spencer Tracy and Katharine Hepburn. While the two became lovers and remained so for years, Tracy never divorced his wife for Hepburn. Their meeting is the stuff of Hollywood legend. When the two were introduced by producer Joseph L. Mankiewicz, Kate declared, "I'm afraid I'm a bit tall for Mr. Tracy." Mankiewicz replied, "Don't worry, he'll cut you down to size."

Right: Spencer Tracy took top billing for *Woman of the Year* (1942) and set the precedent for all his subsequent teamings with Hepburn. When writer Garson Kanin suggested it might be more chivalrous to allow Kate to have first billing, Tracy replied, "Listen chowderhead, a movie isn't a goddamn lifeboat." Still, it was Hepburn, not Tracy, who received an Academy Award nomination (her fourth) for her work on the film.

Below: Hepburn and Tracy preparing for the 1944 CBS radio broadcast of *Woman of the Year.*

Opposite: Kate and Spencer Tracy on the set of *Keeper of the Flame* (1942). During filming, Hepburn made several comments on the actors' performances to director and longtime ally George Cukor, who listened mutely to her suggestions. But finally, when she questioned the believability of a conflagration scene in the script, Cukor shot back, "It must be wonderful to know all about acting and all about fires."

R ight: In the MGM film adaptation of Pearl Buck's novel *Dragon Seed* (1944), Hepburn and other Anglo-Saxon actors, including Walter Hudson as Ling Tan and Hurd Hatfield as Lao San, played Chinese peasants at the time of the Japanese invasion in 1937. The film was shot in Southern California's San Fernando Valley.

ight: *Without Love* originated as a Broadway vehicle for Hepburn in 1942. In 1945 it became the third Tracy-Hepburn film. Their characters are united in a platonic marriage until the last reel of the film. The supporting cast included Keenan Wynn (pictured right), Lucille Ball, and Gloria Grahame.

elow: Tracy and Hepburn in *Without Love.* Director Henry Gerrard said of the two, "The important thing is that I don't coach them on their scenes together. No one should do that, for they do a thorough job by themselves...."

Above: The film *Undercurrent* (1946), in which Hepburn starred opposite Robert Mitchum and Robert Taylor (pictured here), received a lukewarm public and critical reception. *Time* magazine said the film had, "an indigestible plot full of false leads and unkept promises, like a woman's magazine serial consumed all at one gulp."

Left: Kate dines with the director of *Undercurrent,* Vincente Minelli.

Opposite: Katharine poses with artist McClelland Barclay in his New York studio next to the "Spirit of Tolerance" poster for which she was the model.

Above: In 1947, Tracy and Hepburn appeared in MGM's adaptation of Conrad Richter's novel *The Sea of Grass*. Directed by Elia Kazan, the story has Tracy playing a cattle baron obsessively attached to his land. *The New York Times* called Hepburn's performance of Tracy's strong-willed wife, "distressingly pompous and false." Unfortunately at this point in her career, movies other than comedies, particularly movies she did with Spencer Tracy, were not well received by critics.

Below: Hepburn with Paul Henreid in *Song of Love* (1947). *The New Yorker* said, "She behaves throughout as if she had just been wreathed in a Vassar daisy chain, while Paul Henreid, as Schumann, refuses to register anything but torpor."

Left: Hepburn as Clara Schumann in *Song of Love*. When a friend asked her why she didn't break her ties with MGM after the series of poor roles they had handed her, Kate replied, "Ah, yes, but MGM are really wonderful when you're in Chicago and have to change trains."

Below: Hepburn, with her musical advisor Laura Dubman standing by, practices for her role as Clara Schumann, the great pianist and wife of composer Robert Schumann in *Song of Love*.

Right: *Adam's Rib* (1949), the classic George Cukor comedy, is the story of a husband and wife, both lawyers, who find themselves on the opposite sides of the same case. *The New York Times* said of the Hepburn-Tracy pair, "...their perfect compatibility in comic capers is delightful to see."

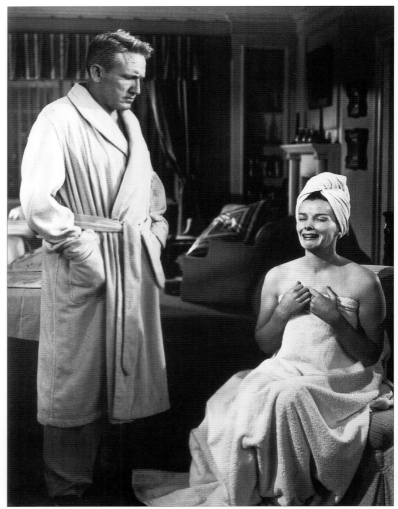

Below: Hepburn received critical praise for her role in *State of the Union* (1949), directed by Frank Capra. However, fellow cast member Adolph Menjou, a then-leader of the pro-McCarthy Hollywood right wing, didn't care for Hepburn or her left-leaning politics. "Scratch a do-gooder like Hepburn and she'll yell Pravda!" he griped. Tracy retorted, "Scratch a Hepburn and what you get is an ass full of buckshot."

Right: Taking a break, both professionally and personally, from Spencer Tracy, Hepburn returned to Broadway to play Rosalind in *As You Like It*. The show toured for nine weeks to ecstatic reviews. She is pictured here with costar William Prince.

Above: In 1951, Kate appeared in what many believe to be her best film performance. Leaving Tracy for Humphrey Bogart (right), MGM for United Artists, George Cukor for John Huston, and Hollywood for Africa, her role as a prim missionary in *The African Queen* won her her fifth Oscar nomination. Bogart won his only Oscar for his performance.

Right: *The African Queen* prompted *Time* magazine to publish a cover story on Hepburn that hailed her as more than just another movie star. "In Kate Hepburn's twenty-four years on stage and screen her detractors have been many, but this year she is stronger than she ever was: by her own estimate she has made more than three million dollars as an actress."

Left: In 1952, Kate finished out her contract with MGM in typical fashion. She starred with Spencer Tracy in the George Cukor–directed comedy, *Pat and Mike,* written by Ruth Gordon and Garson Kanin.

Opposite: Of Kate's performance in the 1952 Broadway production of George Bernard Shaw's *The Millionairess, The New York Herald Tribune* said, "Miss Hepburn is beautiful, radiant, vital and not very good."

ight: Hepburn with director David Lean in Venice during the shooting of *Summertime* (1955). Kate said working with Lean "made a very deep and definite impression on me, and he was one of the most interesting directors I ever worked with."

elow: In *Summertime*, Hepburn played a single teacher who, while vacationing in Italy, falls in love with a man she later learns is married. She received her sixth Oscar nomination for her moving performance.

ight: *The Iron Petticoat* (1956) paired Hepburn with comedian Bob Hope. Shot in London, the film was one of the worst of either star's careers. The screenwriter, Ben Hecht, was so appalled at the final result, he took his name off the credits.

Above: *The Rainmaker* (1956) paired Kate with Burt Lancaster and earned her an Oscar nomination for the seventh time—and her second time in two consecutive years.

Left: Hepburn rehearsing for the opening of Shakespeare's *Merchant of Venice*, by the America Shakespeare Festival at Stratford, Connecticut, in 1957. Hepburn said that the first requirement for playing Shakespeare is "you must be able to speak English and you have to be able to move, not stumble and mumble around like a goon-faced idiot."

Chapter Four

Icon

Above: Katharine Hepburn as Eleanor of Aquitaine in *The Lion in Winter* (1968).

Opposite: After more than twenty years on stage and screen, Hepburn had become a legend in her own time.

Above: Kate with Spencer Tracy in the 1957 film *Desk Set*. Prior to filming, Hepburn nursed Tracy out of one of his many bouts with the bottle. Tracy's alcoholism was interfering with his work and Kate devoted herself to looking after him.

eft: A mock battle of the stars on the set of the motion picture *Suddenly, Last Summer* (1959). Montgomery Clift (left, rear) and director Joseph L. Mankiewicz are at each other's throats while Kate and costar Elizabeth Taylor have it out in the foreground in a stunt for photographers that parodied the many reports of fighting during the production. Nevertheless, Hepburn's final act on the set was to spit in the faces of Mankiewicz and producer Sam Spiegel for the way they treated Clift, who was a substance abuser.

elow: Hepburn with Elizabeth Taylor in *Suddenly, Last Summer.* Both women were nominated for Oscars (though neither won). The film also marked the first time that Kate had accepted billing below another actress.

Kate with Spencer Tracy and Sidney Poitier in *Guess Who's Coming to Dinner* (1967), the story of liberal-minded parents whose ideals are tested when their daughter announces her intention to marry a black man. Directed by Stanley Kramer, the film received ten Oscar nominations and Hepburn took home her second award for Best Actress. The film also marked the end of the Tracy-Hepburn films as it would be the last film of Tracy's career.

Opposite: Hepburn and Tracy during the filming of *Guess Who's Coming to Dinner*. Tracy did not attend the cast and crew party when production wrapped. He told friend Garson Kanin, "Too emotional. This is it. The Big Wrap-Up. I've retired. I thought I might go, but then right after the last shot today Stanley said, 'That's the one!' And I knew it was over and we shook hands and he started to cry and so did I and I figured the hell with it and came home." He died two weeks later.

Above: Kate's niece Katharine Houghton (right) made her screen debut as Kate's daughter in *Guess Who's Coming to Dinner*.

elow: Hepburn as Eleanor of Aquitaine and Peter O'Toole as Henry II of England in the 1968 film, *The Lion in Winter.* Both O'Toole and Hepburn were nominated for Oscars for their performances. For Kate it was an unprecedented eleventh nomination and her third victory.

Above: Kate playing cricket on the set of *The Lion in Winter*. Her costar Peter O'Toole called her a cross between Medusa and Tugboat Annie. Director Anthony Harvey said, "Working with her is like going to Paris at the age of seventeen and finding everything is the way you thought it would be."

Left: At the age of sixty-two, Hepburn (here with Gail Dixon) took on her first musical role, as fashion designer Gabrielle "Coco" Chanel in the Broadway production of *Coco* (1970). She accepted the role "...because it's the first time in my life anyone wanted me for my voice." At the time, it was the most expensive Broadway musical ever and as long as Hepburn starred, it was successful, selling out every performance. She even garnered a Tony nomination.

Opposite: Hepburn in the 1969 film *The Madwoman of Chaillot*. Director John Huston shot the first seventeen days then quit over script quarrels. While visually beautiful, the film was ultimately a star-studded mishmash.

Right: Hepburn as Hecuba, the Greek queen of Troy, in the 1971 Michael Cacoyannis production of Euripides' *The Trojan Women*.

Above: Two legends meet. Hepburn played opposite John Wayne in *Rooster Cogburn,* the 1974 sequel to Wayne's Oscar-winning film *True Grit* (1969).

Right: (left to right) Strother Martin, Hepburn, and Wayne in *Rooster Cogburn.* Said Wayne, "She's the best.... Bogey and Spence would sure envy me now."

Above: Kate and George Cukor at the 1978 Avery Fisher Hall Gala honoring Cukor, New York City.

Right: Kate, Sir Laurence Olivier, and director George Cukor on the set of *Love Among the Ruins*, a 1975 ABC made-for-television movie. Olivier and Hepburn both won Emmys for their performances. Although Kate had been a witness at Olivier's marriage to Vivien Leigh, he had dreaded appearing with Hepburn, thinking she would be a temperamental prima donna, but they got along famously.

elow: A scene from *The Corn Is Green*, a 1979 CBS television movie directed by the then seventy-nine-year-old George Cukor. This would be the tenth—and last—collaboration between Hepburn and the director, who had cast her in her first film.

Above: Playwright Ernest Thompson on stage with Kate after the opening of *West Side Waltz* (1981). *The New York Times* wrote, "I'm not sure that author Ernest Thompson realizes...what small miracles Katharine Hepburn is bestowing on his play....There may have been a time when she coasted on mannerisms, turned on her rhythms into a form of rapid transit. That time is long gone."

Left: Fans and heavy security surround Hepburn as she leaves the Barrymore Theater in New York City after her opening performance in *West Side Waltz*.

eft: In 1982's *On Golden Pond*, Hepburn starred with Henry Fonda in his last performance. The actor's daughter, Jane Fonda, played his alienated screen-daughter, and produced the film as an homage to her father. Henry Fonda, Kate, and screenwriter Ernest Thompson all won Oscars for the film.

elow: Kate with Nick Nolte in the 1985 film *The Ultimate Solution of Grace Quigley*. The film told the story of a lonely elderly woman (Hepburn) who hires a hit man (Nolte) to end her life.

Opposite: In 1986, Hepburn hosted a television special "Spencer Tracy: A Tribute by Katharine Hepburn." She said, "He was a great actor—simple. He could just do it. Never overdone. Just perfection. There was no complication. The performance was unguarded. He could make you laugh. He could make you cry. He could listen."

Always a good interview, Kate speaks candidly with Dick Cavett (above) and Barbara Walters (left).

Above: "Self-sacrificing women give me melancholia. One thing is certain, whether I'm affable or difficult, I always have a good time," stated Hepburn in an interview for *McCall's*. She was named their first "Woman of the Year" in 1970.

Below: Kennedy Center honorees (left to right) Billy Wilder, Katharine Hepburn, and Dizzy Gillespie at the White House, Washington, D.C.

Left: In 1988, Hepburn appeared at a tribute to herself and her mother, hosted by the Planned Parenthood Federation.

Above: An unstoppable Kate onstage and on crutches at Radio City Music Hall for the "Night of 100 Stars" (1990).

Left: In a special two-part 1991 interview with the *Today* show's Katie Couric, Hepburn openly discussed her life, career, and long-standing love affair with Spencer Tracy.

Epilogue

Left: By the 1950s, Hepburn had done something utterly uncommon for a Hollywood actress: she had shaped herself and her career independent of any studio.

Opposite: Katharine Hepburn, the "Hollywood Yankee."

The Hollywood in which Katharine Hepburn rose to stardom was indeed in its "Golden Age." In her 1991 autobiography entitled *Me*, Hepburn described director George Cukor's palatial residence and the parties she would attend there during this time. She wrote of a cushioned couch: "Here we had our drinks on great occasions. There we were all tumbled together, the seat so deep you couldn't get out once you got in. Stravinsky, Ethel Barrymore, Edith Sitwell, the Goldwyns, Hugh Walpole, Somerset Maugham, Sir Osbert Sitwell, Groucho Marx, Ina Claire,

Gregory Peck, Fanny Brice, Judy Garland, Natasha Paley, Larry Olivier, Vivien Leigh, Noel Willman. Well, you name them, Gar Kanin, Ruth Gordon, anyone who was."

Among such a diverse and talented group of luminaries, Hepburn held her own. Her forceful personality, unique beauty, and tremendous talent made her not just a product of, but an element essential to, Hollywood's most successful era. She became a film icon, with a career spanning over sixty years. In 1994, at the age of eighty-eight, she appeared with Warren Beatty and Annette Bening in the remake of the 1939 Leo McCarey film *Love Affair*.

Katharine married once, at an early age, was divorced, and never married again. She had no children. While she had romances with the likes of Howard Hughes and John Ford, the only man she claimed to have ever really loved was Spencer Tracy, who remained married to someone else throughout their involvement. She wrote, "I have no idea how Spence felt about me. I can only say I think that if he hadn't liked me he wouldn't have hung around. As simple as that. He wouldn't talk about it and I didn't talk about it. We just passed twenty-seven years together in what was to me absolute bliss. It is called LOVE."

About her profession, Hepburn said, "A lot of hogwash is talked about acting. It's not all that fancy.... Spencer Tracy always said acting was 'learn your lines and get on with it.' So [did] Larry Olivier and John Gielgud, all the great ones." She continued, "Life's what's important. Walking, houses, family. Birth and pain and joy. And then death." Hepburn has said, "When I close the book, I'll never think I've been an actress." Yet it is through her acting that Katharine Hepburn will live forever.

Filmography

MOTION PICTURES

Love Affair. Warner Bros. (1994)

George Stevens: A Filmmaker's Journey. Castle Rock (1984)

Grace Quigley. Cannon/MGM/United Artists (1984) (a.k.a. *The Ultimate Solution of Grace Quigley* [1985])

On Golden Pond. Universal (1981)*

Olly, Olly, Oxen Free. Sanrio (1978) (a.k.a. *The Great Balloon Adventure; The Great Balloon Race*)

Rooster Cogburn. Universal (1975) (a.k.a. *Rooster Cogburn...and the Lady*)

The Trojan Women. Cinerama/Joseph Shaftel (1971)

The Madwoman of Chaillot. United/Warner Bros. (1969)

The Lion in Winter. Martin Poll/Avco Embassy (1968)**

Guess Who's Coming to Dinner. Stanley Kramer Prods./Columbia (1967)**

Long Day's Journey Into Night. Embassy (1962)*

Suddenly, Last Summer. Horizon Ltd. in assoc. with Academy Pictures and Camp Films/Columbia (1959)*

Desk Set. 20th Century Fox (1957) (a.k.a. *His Other Woman*)

The Iron Petticoat. Ben Har/MGM (1956) (a.k.a. *Not For Money*)

The Rainmaker. Paramount (1956)*

Summertime. Lopert Film/United Artists (1955)* (a.k.a. *Summer Madness*)

Pat and Mike. MGM (1952)

The African Queen. Horizon-Romulus/United Artists (1951)*

Adam's Rib. MGM (1949)

State of the Union. Liberty Film/MGM (1948) (a.k.a. *The World and His Wife*)

Song of Love. MGM (1947)

The Sea of Grass. MGM (1947)

Undercurrent. MGM (1946)

Without Love. MGM (1945)

Dragon Seed. MGM (1944)

Stage Door Canteen. United Artists (1943)

Keeper of the Flame. MGM (1942)

Woman of the Year. MGM (1942)*

Women in Defense. Government Film (1941)

The Philadelphia Story. MGM (1940)*

Holiday. Columbia (1938) (a.k.a. *Free to Live; Unconventional Linda*)

Bringing Up Baby. RKO (1938)

Stage Door. RKO (1937)

Quality Street. RKO (1937)

A Woman Rebels. RKO (1936)

Mary of Scotland. RKO (1936)

Sylvia Scarlett. RKO (1935)

Alice Adams. RKO (1935)*

Break of Hearts. RKO (1935)

The Little Minister. RKO (1934)

Spitfire. RKO (1934)

Little Women. RKO (1933)

Morning Glory. RKO (1933)**

Christopher Strong. RKO (1933)

A Bill of Divorcement. RKO (1932)

* denotes Academy Award nomination

** denotes Academy Award

TELEVISION

One Christmas (1994)

This Can't Be Love (1994)

Katharine Hepburn: All About Me (1992)

The Man Upstairs (1992)

Laura Lansing Slept Here (1988)

Mrs. Delafield Wants to Marry (1986)

The Corn Is Green (1979)

Love Among the Ruins (1975)

A Delicate Balance (1973)

The Glass Menagerie (1973)

Bibliography

Anderson, Christopher. *Young Kate.* New York: Henry Holt & Company, Inc. 1988

Bryson, John. *The Private World of Katharine Hepburn.* Boston: Little Brown & Company, Inc. 1990

Carey, Gary. *Katharine Hepburn, A Hollywood Yankee.* New York: St. Martin's Press. 1983

Edwards, Anne. *A Remarkable Woman, A Biography of Katharine Hepburn.* New York: William Morrow & Company, Inc. 1985

Freedland, Michael. *Katharine Hepburn.* London: W.H. Allen. 1984

Hepburn, Katharine. *The Making of the African Queen, or How I Went to Africa with Bogart, Bacall and Huston and Almost Lost My Mind.* New York: Alfred A. Knopf. 1987

Hepburn, Katharine. *Me.* New York: Alfred A. Knopf, 1991

Hingham, Charles. *Kate: The Life of Katharine Hepburn.* New York: W.W. Norton & Company, Inc. 1975

Leaming, Barbara. *Katharine Hepburn.* New York: Crown Publishers, 1995

Marill, Alvin. *Katharine Hepburn: A Pyramid Illustrated History of the Movies.* New York: Pyramid Publications, 1973

Morley, Sheridan. *Katharine Hepburn.* Boston: Little, Brown & Company, 1984

Peebles Press International. *Katharine Hepburn: In The Spotlight.* New York: Galley Press, 1980

Index

Photography Credits

Archive Photos: pp. 18, 36, 42, 50, 66 bottom, 82 bottom

Corbis-Bettmann: pp. 17, 59 bottom, 63 bottom

The Everett Collection: pp. 14, 21 top, 24 top, 29, 38, 45, 54-55, 63 top, 69 top, 81 bottom, 83 bottom, 88, 89 both, 91 bottom left

©Ron Galella: pp. 83 top, 85 bottom, 91 right

The Kobal Collection: pp. 2, 6, 8, 10, 11, 13, 25, 30 bottom, 44 both, 49, 51 bottom, 53, 56 bottom, 60, 64 bottom, 65, 66 top, 67, 78, 80, 81 top, 84, 86-87 left, 90 top

The Museum of Modern Art: pp. 9, 12, 15 top, 19, 20, 21 bottom, 22, 23, 24 bottom, 26-27 left, 27 right, 28, 31, 32 bottom, 33, 34, 37 both, 39, 40 top, 41, 43 both, 47, 48, 51 top, 52, 56 top, 57 both, 58 top, 59 top, 61, 62-63 left, 64 top, 64 left, 68 top left, 68 bottom, 73 bottom

Penguin/Corbis-Bettmann: p. 77

Personality Photos: pp. 74-75, 93

Photofest: p. 46

Retna, Ltd.: ©Holland: pp. 35, 92; ©Doc Pele/Stills: pp. 58 bottom, 70, 71, 72, 82 top; ©Alban: 87 right

Reuters/Corbis-Bettmann: p. 90 bottom

Springer/Corbis-Bettmann: pp. 16 top

UPI/Corbis-Bettmann: pp. 15 bottom left, 15 bottom right, 16 bottom, 30 top, 32 top, 40 bottom, 68 top right, 69 bottom, 73 top, 76, 79, 85 top, 91 top left